DEVOTIONS
FOR
PATIENCE
&WHOLENESS

JOB & COLOSSIANS

DEVOTIONS
FOR
PATIENCE
& WHOLENESS

JOB & COLOSSIANS

Warren W. Wiersbe

HONOR HB BOOKS

Inspiration and Motivation for the Seasons of Life

COOK COMMUNICATIONS MINISTRIES
Colorado Springs, Colorado • Paris, Ontario
KINGSWAY COMMUNICATIONS LTD
Eastbourne, England

Honor Books® is an imprint of
Cook Communications Ministries, Colorado Springs, CO 80918
Cook Communications, Paris, Ontario
Kingsway Communications, Eastbourne, England

DEVOTIONS FOR PATIENCE AND WHOLENESS
© 2006 by Warren W. Wiersbe

Cover Design: Jackson Design CO, LLC/Greg Jackson

First Printing, 2006
Printed in the United States of America

1 2 3 4 5 6 7 8 9 10 Printing/Year 10 09 08 07 06

Unless otherwise noted, Scripture quotations are taken from the HOLY
BIBLE, NEW INTERNATIONAL VERSION®. Copyright © 1973, 1978,
1984 by International Bible Society. Used by permission of Zondervan.
All rights reserved. Scripture quotations marked (KJV) are taken from the
King James Version of the Bible. (Public Domain); Scriptures marked
(TLB) are taken from *The Living Bible,* © 1971, Tyndale House Publishers,
Wheaton, IL 60189. Used by permission; and Scriptures marked *The New
Testament: An Expanded Translation* (Wuest) by Kenneth S. Wuest © 1961
by the Wm. B. Eerdmans Publishing Company, used by permission.
Italics in Scripture have been added by the author for emphasis.

This book was originally published as two paperback editions in 1994
and 1995, compiled by Stan Campbell. Each devotional reading is
adapted from Warren Wiersbe's "Be" series.

Library of Congress Cataloging-in-Publication Data

Wiersbe, Warren W.
   Devotions for patience and wholeness : Job and Colossians / Warren
Wiersbe.
       p. cm. -- (60 days in the Word)
   Includes bibliographical references and index.
   ISBN 1-56292-702-7 (alk. paper)
   1. Bible. O.T. Job--Meditations. 2. Bible. N.T. Colossians--Meditations. I.
Title.
   BS1415.54.W54 2006
   242'.2--dc22

                                          2005026493

Patience

Thirty Daily Readings from the Book of Job

The only thing many of us know about patience is how to spell the word.

The book of Job is the greatest book ever written on patience. Nobody in Bible history, except Jesus Christ, suffered more than Job, and because Job suffered, we can learn from him how to accept the tough experiences of life and profit from them. As we listen to Job's debates with his friends and then hear the penetrating words of Jehovah, we can discover new depths of understanding about life and new facets of truth about ourselves. Through it all, we can learn how to develop patience.

What life does *to* us depends on what life finds *in* us. The book of Job challenges us to have faith in our hearts that the trials of life are appointments, not accidents, and that God does indeed work all things together for our good (Rom. 8:28 KJV). When God puts us into the furnace, He keeps His eye on the clock and His hand on the thermostat, so we don't have to be afraid.

One more thing: Whenever we ask God for patience, He usually sends trials. Be prepared. There are no shortcuts when it comes to building Christian character. But it is worth it to go through the furnace of suffering if, like Job, we can say, "Though he slay me, yet will I hope in him!" (Job 13:15). When that is our testimony, we will come out of the furnace as pure gold.

That is what happened to Job (23:10), and it can happen to *you*.

The Lord gave and the Lord has taken away;
may the name of the Lord be praised.

Job 1:21

Day 1

Ready to Suffer?

Read James 5:11

You have heard of Job's perseverance and have seen what the Lord finally brought about. The Lord is full of compassion and mercy.

JAMES 5:11

Many people have *heard* about Job and his trials, but not many people *understand* what those trials were all about and what God was trying to accomplish through them. Nor do they realize that Job suffered as he did so that God's people today might learn from his experiences how to be patient in suffering and endure to the end.

When I decided to write about Job, I said to my wife, "I wonder how much suffering we'll have to go through so I can write this book." Little did we realize the trials that God would permit us to experience! But we can testify that God is faithful, He answers prayer, and He always has a wonderful purpose in mind (Jer. 29:11).

You, too, may have to go through the furnace in order to study the book of Job and really grasp its message. If so, don't be afraid! By faith, just say with Job, "He knows the way that I take; when he has tested me, I will come forth as gold" (Job 23:10). God fears no fire. Whatever you have that is burned up and left behind in the furnace isn't worth having anyway.

As we study the book of Job together, I trust that two things will be accomplished in your life: You will learn to be patient in your own trials, and you will learn how to help others in their trials. Your world is filled with people who need encouragement, and God may be preparing you for just that ministry. Either way, I hope this book helps you.

Applying God's Truth:

1. What are some current situations you are facing that are causing you to suffer?

2. On a scale of 1 (least) to 10 (most), how severely would you say you have suffered in the past? What events have caused the most intense suffering?

3. What do you hope to discover as you go through the book of Job?

Day 2

Gritty Integrity

Read Job 1:1–5

> *In the land of Uz there lived a man whose name was Job. This man was blameless and upright; he feared God and shunned evil.*
>
> JOB 1:1

Lord Byron was on target when he wrote: "Truth is always strange; stranger than fiction."

The book of Job is not religious fiction. Job was a real person, not an imaginary character; both Ezekiel (14:14, 20) and James (5:11) attest to that fact. Because he was a real man who had real experiences, he can tell us what we need to know about life and its problems in this real world.

Job was "blameless and upright." He was not sinless, for nobody can claim that distinction except Jesus, but he was complete and mature in character and "straight" in conduct. The Hebrew word translated "blameless" is related to "integrity," another important word used throughout the book of Job. People with integrity are whole persons, without hypocrisy or duplicity. In the face of his friends' accusations and God's silence, Job maintained his integrity; and the Lord ultimately vindicated him.

The foundation for Job's character was the fact that he "feared God and shunned evil." To fear the Lord means to respect who He is, what He says, and what He does. It is not the cringing fear of a slave before a master, but the loving reverence of a child before a father, a respect that leads to obedience. "The remarkable thing about fearing

God," said Oswald Chambers, "is that when you fear God you fear nothing else, whereas if you do not fear God you fear everything else."

Applying God's Truth:

1. What things would you need to do before other people considered you blameless?

2. Can you think of a recent situation in which you considered compromising your integrity? If not, can you think of any situation in which you *might?*

3. Would you say that you fear God? Explain.

Day 3

First, the Bad News

Read Job 1:6–19

> *Yet another messenger came and said, "Your sons and daughters were feasting ... when suddenly a mighty wind swept in from the desert and struck the four corners of the house. It collapsed on them and they are dead."*
>
> JOB 1:18–19

In one day, Job was stripped of his wealth. One after another, four frightened messengers reported that five hundred yoke of oxen, five hundred donkeys, and three thousand camels were stolen in enemy raids; seven thousand sheep were struck by lightning and killed; and all ten of his children were killed in a windstorm (vv. 13–19).

Job knew *what* had happened, but he did not know *why* it had happened, and that is the crux of the matter. Because the author allows us to visit the throne room of heaven and hear God and Satan speak, we know who caused the destruction and why he was allowed to cause it (vv. 6–12). But if we did not have this insight, we would probably take the same approach as Job's friends and blame Job for the tragedy.

Several important truths emerge from this scene, not the least of which is that *God is sovereign in all things.* He is on the throne of heaven, the angels do His will and report to Him, and even Satan can do nothing to God's people without God's permission. "The Almighty" is one of the key names for God in Job; it is used thirty-one times. From the outset, the writer reminds us that, no matter what happens in this world and in our lives, God is on the throne and has everything under control. We may not know until we get to heaven why God allowed certain things to happen. Meanwhile, we walk by faith and say with Job, "May the name of the LORD be praised" (v. 21).

Applying God's Truth:

1. If the devastating events of Job's life happened to you today, what do you think you would do? Be specific.

2. How would these events make you feel about God? (Be truthful.)

3. When you get to heaven, what is one thing you would like to ask God about?

Day 4

Worst of Times, Worship Times

Read Job 1:20–22

> *The LORD gave and the LORD has taken away;*
> *may the name of the LORD be praised.*
>
> JOB 1:21

The hosts of heaven and of hell watched to see how Job would respond to the loss of his wealth and his children. He expressed his grief in a manner normal for that day, for God expects us to be human (1 Thess. 4:13). After all, even Jesus wept (John 11:35). But then Job worshipped God and uttered a profound statement of faith.

First, he looked back to his birth: "Naked I came from my mother's womb" (Job 1:21). Everything Job owned was given to him by God, and the same God who gave it had the right to take it away. Job simply acknowledged that he was a steward.

Then Job looked ahead to his death: "And naked I will depart" (v. 21). He would not return to his mother's womb, because that would be impossible. He would go to "Mother Earth," be buried, and return to dust. Nothing he had acquired between his birth and death would go with him into the next world.

Finally, Job looked up and uttered a magnificent statement of faith: "The LORD gave and the LORD has taken away; may the name of the LORD be praised" (v. 21). Instead of cursing God, as Satan said Job would do (vv. 9–11), Job blessed the Lord! Anybody can say, "The Lord gave" or "The Lord has taken away"; but it takes real faith to say in the midst of sorrow and suffering, "May the name of the Lord be praised."

Applying God's Truth:

1. Do you think Job's worship during his great tragedy suggests that he was in denial of his situation? Explain.

2. Do you think Job's actions were appropriate? Why or why not?

3. What are some less effective responses to tragedy that people use today?

Day 5

Three Heads Are No Better Than One

Read Job 2—3

> *When Job's three friends ... heard about all the troubles that had come upon him, they set out from their homes and met together by agreement to go and sympathize with him and comfort him.*
>
> JOB 2:11

We will be spending a good deal of time with Job's three friends, so we had better get acquainted with them.

All three of the men were old (32:6), older than Job (15:10), but we assume that *Eliphaz* was the oldest. He is named first (2:11), he spoke first (4:1), and the Lord seemed to have accepted him as the elder member of the trio (42:7). Eliphaz put great faith in tradition (15:18–19), and the God he worshipped was an inflexible Lawgiver. He had a rigid theology that left little or no room for the grace of God.

Bildad must have been the second oldest of the three since he is named second and spoke after Eliphaz (8:1). In a word, Bildad was a legalist. For some reason, Bildad was sure that Job's children had died because they also were sinners (v. 4). The man seemed to have no feeling for his hurting friend.

Zophar was the youngest of the three (2:11) and surely the most dogmatic. He speaks like a schoolmaster addressing a group of ignorant freshmen. "Know this!" is his unfeeling approach. He is merciless and tells Job that God is giving him far less than he deserves for his sins (11:6)! Interestingly enough, Zophar speaks to Job only twice. Either he decides he is unable to answer Job's arguments or feels that it is a waste of time trying to help Job.

All three men said some good and true things, as well as some foolish things; but they were of no help to Job because their viewpoint was too narrow. These men perfectly illustrate Dorothy Sayers' statement, "There's nothing you can't prove if your outlook is only sufficiently limited."

Applying God's Truth:

1. When you have serious problems, what three friends do you most trust for advice?

2. Do you have "friends" like Job's, who offer advice with little, if any, sensitivity? How do you respond to their advice?

3. What can *you* learn about being a friend from Eliphaz, Bildad, and Zophar?

Day 6

A Word from the Unwise

Read Job 4—5

*Then Eliphaz the Temanite replied: "If someone ventures a word with you,
will you be impatient? But who can keep from speaking?"*

Job 4:1–2

Job's three friends were silent for seven days (2:13), and Job later
wished they had stayed that way (13:5). Then Eliphaz the Temanite
answered Job. But what did he answer? The pain in Job's heart? No,
he answered the words from Job's lips, *and this was a mistake*. A wise
counselor and comforter must listen with the heart and respond to
feelings as well as to words. We do not heal a broken heart with logic;
we heal a broken heart with love. Yes, we must speak the truth, but
we must be sure to speak the truth in love (Eph. 4:15).

Eliphaz's approach seemed to start out positive enough, even gen-
tle, but it was only honey to prepare Job for the bitterness that would
follow. "Don't get upset, Job!" is what he was saying. "In the past your
words have been a help to many people, and we want our words to be
a help to you" (Job 4:4–6, author's paraphrase).

We must never underestimate the power of words to encourage
people in the battles of life. James Moffatt translates Job 4:4, "Your
words have kept men on their feet." The right words spoken at the
right time and with the right motive can make a tremendous difference in the lives of others. Our words can nourish those who are weak
and encourage those who are defeated. But our words can also hurt

those who are broken and only add to their burdens, so we must be careful what we say and how we say it.

Applying God's Truth:

1. What do you suppose Job's friends were thinking during their seven days of silence?

2. Can you think of a recent time when you responded to someone's *words* rather than that person's *feelings?* How might you have improved your response?

3. When have you felt that you had the right words, at the right time, and with the right motive—and helped or comforted someone a great deal?

Day 7

Defending Justice, Forgetting Love

Read Job 6—8

> *Then Bildad the Shuhite replied: "How long will you say such things?*
> *Your words are a blustering wind."*
>
> JOB 8:1–2

"Your words are a blustering wind." Can you imagine a counselor saying that to a suffering individual who wanted to die? Bildad did; in fact, he used the same approach in his next speech (18:2). Job had poured out his grief and was waiting to hear a sympathetic word, but his friend said that Job's speech was just so much hot air.

There is a reason for Bildad's approach: He was so concerned about defending the justice of God that he forgot the needs of his friend. While Bildad's theology was correct—God *is* just—his application of that theology was wrong. Bildad was looking at only one aspect of God's nature—His holiness and justice—and had forgotten His love, mercy, and goodness. Yes, "God is light" (1 John 1:5); but we must not forget that "God is love" (4:8, 16). His love is a holy love, and His holiness is exercised in love, even when He judges sin.

How are these two attributes of God reconciled? At the cross. When Jesus died for the sins of the world, the righteousness of God was vindicated, for sin was judged; but the love of God was demonstrated, for a Savior was provided. At Calvary, God was revealed as both "just and the one who justifies" (Rom. 3:26). God's law said, "The soul who sins is the one who will die" (Ezek. 18:4, 20); and God obeyed His own law in the sacrificing of His Son on the cross. In

Christ's resurrection, the grace of God triumphed over sin and death, and all who repent of their sins and trust Jesus Christ will be saved (Acts 2:21; Rom. 10:9–10).

Applying God's Truth:

1. What problems might people expect if they focus too much on God's justice without considering His great love?

2. What problems might people expect if they concentrate on God's love while excluding His holy justice?

3. What steps can you take to ensure that you maintain a sense of God's love *and* justice as you advise and console others?

Day 8

An Offering of Suffering

Read Job 9—10

> *Though I were innocent, I could not answer him;*
> *I could only plead with my Judge for mercy.*
>
> JOB 9:15

In Job 9 and 10, Job asks three questions: (1) "How can I be right-eous before God?" (9:1–13); (2) "How can I meet God in court?" (vv. 14–35); and (3) "Why was I born?" (10:1–22). You can see how these questions connect. Job is righteous, but he has to prove it. How can a mortal man prove himself righteous before God? Can he take God to court? But if God doesn't step in and testify on Job's behalf, what is the purpose of all this suffering? Why was Job even born?

Job could not understand what God was doing, *and it was impor-tant that he not understand.* Had Job known that God was using him as a weapon to defeat Satan, he could have simply sat back and waited trustfully for the battle to end. But as Job surveyed himself and his sit-uation, he asked the same question the disciples asked when Mary anointed the Lord Jesus with expensive perfume: "Why this waste?" (Mark 14:4; John 11:2). Before we criticize Job too severely, let's recall how many times we have asked that question ourselves when a baby has died or a promising young person has been killed in an accident.

Nothing that is given to Christ in faith and love is ever wasted. The fragrance of Mary's ointment faded from the scene centuries ago, but the significance of her worship has blessed Christians in every age and continues to do so (Mark 14:6–9). Job was bankrupt and sick, and all he could give to the Lord was his suffering by faith; *but that is just what God wanted in order to silence the Devil.*

Applying God's Truth:

1. With what top three questions about life and God are *you* currently struggling?

2. Can you think of an event in the past when you couldn't understand what God was doing (or why) but later were able to see His plan clearly?

3. Mary offered ointment. Job offered suffering. Can you think of something equally unusual or unique to offer God?

Day 9

Zophar, So Good?

Read Job 11

> *If you put away the sin that is in your hand and allow*
> *no evil to dwell in your tent, then you will lift up your face*
> *without shame; you will stand firm and without fear.*
>
> JOB 11:14–15

Zophar makes three accusations against Job: Job is guilty of sin (vv. 1–4); Job is ignorant of God (vv. 5–12); and Job is stubborn in his refusal to repent (vv. 13–20). "There is hope!" is Zophar's encouraging word to Job, and he describes what Job can experience. But if Job wants these blessings, he has to get them on Zophar's terms. Yes, there is hope, but it is hope with a condition attached to it: Job must repent and confess his sins (vv. 13–14). *Zophar is tempting Job to bargain with God so he can get out of his troubles.* This is exactly what Satan wanted Job to do!

"Does Job fear God for nothing?" Satan asked (1:9). Satan accused Job of having a "commercial faith" that promised prosperity in return for obedience. If Job had followed Zophar's advice, he would have played right into the hands of the Enemy.

Job did not have a "commercial faith" that made bargains with God. He had a confident faith that said, "Though he slay me, yet will I hope in him" (13:15). That doesn't sound like a man looking for an easy way out of difficulties. "Job did not understand the Lord's reasons," said Charles Haddon Spurgeon, "but he continued to confide in His goodness." That is faith!

‹❦›

Applying God's Truth:

1. What have people recently accused you of? How did each accusation make you feel?

2. In what ways do people today attempt to bargain with God?

3. How would you feel in Job's place after hearing the accusations and advice of Zophar?

Day 10

Appealing to a Higher Court

Read Job 12—14

> *Though he slay me, yet will I hope in him;*
> *I will surely defend my ways to his face.*
>
> JOB 13:15

Job 13:13–17 is one of the greatest declarations of faith found anywhere in Scripture, but it must be understood in its context. In it Job is saying to his friends, "I will take my case directly to God and prove my integrity. I know I am taking my life in my hands in approaching God, because He is able to slay me. But if He doesn't slay me, it is proof that I am not the hypocrite you say I am." Later, Job will take an oath and challenge God to pass judgment (Job 27). To approach God personally was a great act of faith, but Job was so sure of his integrity that he would take his chances. After all, if he did nothing, he would die; and if he was rejected by God, he would die; but there was always the possibility that God would prove him right.

Why does Job want to meet God in court? So that God can once and for all state His "case" against Job and let Job know the sins in his life that have caused him to suffer so much. "Why should God pay so much attention to me?" asks Job. "He treats me like an enemy, but I'm just a weak leaf in the wind, a piece of chaff that is worth nothing. I'm a piece of rotting wood and a moth-eaten garment, yet God treats me like a prisoner of war and watches me every minute" (13:24–28, author's paraphrase). Job felt the time had come to settle the matter, even if it meant losing his own life in the process.

Applying God's Truth:

1. What do you think about Job's desire to meet God "in court"?

2. Have you ever felt so righteous and innocent that you would invite God to "check you out" personally? Explain.

3. What do you think motivated Job's actions: Desperation? Confidence? Or something else?

Day 11

You Get What You Deserve?

Read Job 15

All his days the wicked man suffers torment,
the ruthless through all the years stored up for him.

JOB 15:20

In his first speech, Eliphaz had described the blessings of the godly (5:17–26); but now he describes the sufferings of the ungodly. The problem with Eliphaz's statement about the judgment of the wicked is that *it is not always true in this life*. Many wicked people go through life apparently happy and successful, while many godly people experience suffering and seeming failure. It is true that *ultimately* the wicked suffer and the godly are blessed, but, meanwhile, it often looks like the situation is reversed (Ps. 73; Jer. 12:1–4). Furthermore, God gives sunshine to the evil and the good and sends rain on the just and the unjust (Matt. 5:45). He is long suffering toward sinners (2 Peter 3:9) and waits for His goodness to lead them to repentance (Rom. 2:4; Luke 15:17–19).

The greatest judgment God could send to the wicked in this life would be to *let them have their own way, saying*: "They have received their reward" (Matt. 6:2, 5, 16). The only heaven the godless will know is the enjoyment they have on earth in this life, and God is willing for them to have it. The only suffering the godly will experience is in this life, for in heaven there will be no pain or tears (Rev. 7:17; 21:4). Furthermore, the suffering that God's people experience now is working *for* them and will one day lead to glory (1 Peter 1:6–8; 5:10; 2 Cor.

4:16–18; Rom. 8:18). Eliphaz and his friends had the situation all confused.

Applying God's Truth:

1. Do you ever agree with Eliphaz's opinion, expressed in today's key verse? Why?

2. How many righteous people do you know who are experiencing major suffering? How about wicked people who seem to be prospering?

3. The next time *you* suffer unfairly, what can you remember to help you endure the situation?

Day 12

Nothing Left to Live For

Read Job 16—17

If the only home I hope for is the grave ... where then is my hope?
JOB 17:13, 15

Job's friends were against him and would not go to court and "post bond" for him (17:3–5). People treated Job as if he were the scum of the earth (v. 6). His body was only the shadow of what it had been (v. 7), and all of his plans had been shattered (v. 11). His friends would not change their minds and come to his defense (v. 10). In fact, they would not face his situation honestly, but they kept telling him that the light would soon dawn for him (v. 12). Is it any wonder that Job saw in death the only way of escape?

God did not answer Job's plea for death because He had something far better planned for him. God looked beyond Job's depression and bitterness and saw that he still had faith. When I was a young pastor, I heard an experienced saint say, "I have lived long enough to be thankful for unanswered prayer." At the time, I was shocked by the statement, but now that I have lived a few more years myself, I know what she was talking about. In the darkness of despair and the prison of pain, we often say things that we later regret, *but God understands all about it and lovingly turns a deaf ear to our words but a tender eye to our wounds.*

Applying God's Truth:

1. Have you ever felt that you had little if anything to live for? If so, what were the circumstances? If not, what is the worst you have ever felt (emotionally)?

2. How could Job's friends have affected his outlook in a more positive way?

3. Can you think of an unanswered prayer in your past for which you are now thankful?

Day 13

Fear as a Motivator

Read Job 18

The lamp of the wicked is snuffed out; the flame of his fire stops burning.
JOB 18:5

In Bildad's second speech, his weapon was *fear*. If the three friends could not reason with Job, or shame Job into repenting, perhaps they could frighten Job by describing what happens when wicked people die. However, Bildad made two mistakes when he gave this speech about the horrors of death. To begin with, he preached it to the wrong man, for Job was already a believer (1:1, 8). Second, he preached it with the wrong motive, for there was no love in his heart. Dr. R. W. Dale, the British preacher, once asked evangelist D. L. Moody if he ever used "the element of terror" in his preaching. Moody replied that he usually preached one sermon on heaven and one on hell in each of his campaigns, but that a "man's heart ought to be very tender" when preaching about the doom of the lost. Bildad did not have a "very tender" heart.

Though Bildad was talking to the wrong man and with the wrong motive, what he said about death should be taken seriously. Death is an enemy to be feared by all who are not prepared to die (Heb. 2:14–15; 1 Cor. 15:26), and the only way to be prepared is to trust Jesus Christ (John 5:24).

For the Christian, death means going home to the Father in heaven (John 14:1–6), falling asleep on earth and waking up in heaven (Acts 7:60; Phil. 1:21–23), entering into rest (Rev. 14:13), and moving into greater light (Prov. 4:18). None of the pictures Bildad used (Job 18:5–21) should be applied to those who have trusted the Lord for salvation.

Applying God's Truth:

1. Has anyone ever tried to use fear as a motivator to attempt to scare you into being a better person or a better Christian? How well did the attempt work?

2. What are some other "motivators" people use with wrong motives?

3. Think of your own recent interactions with friends and family members. Can you think of any instances in which you have tried to influence others with improper motives or tactics?

Day 14

Darkness on a Dead-End Street

Read Job 19:1–20

> *He has blocked my way so I cannot pass;*
> *he has shrouded my paths in darkness.*
> JOB 19:8

Job saw himself as a traveler fenced in. Satan had complained that God had "walled in" Job and his family so that they were protected from trouble (1:9–12). Here Job was complaining because God had blocked his path, and he could not move. He could not see what lay ahead because God had shrouded the way with darkness.

At times God permits His children to experience darkness on a dead-end street where they don't know which way to turn. When this happens to you, *wait for the Lord to give you light in His own time.* Don't try to manufacture your own light or to borrow light from others.

Dr. Bob Jones Sr. used to say, "Never doubt in the darkness what God has taught you in the light." In fact, what God teaches us in the light will become even more meaningful in the darkness.

"Oh, the unspeakable benediction of the 'treasures of darkness'!" wrote Oswald Chambers. "It is not the days of sunshine and splendor and liberty and light that leave their lasting and indelible effect upon the soul, but those nights of the Spirit in which, shadowed by God's hand, hidden in the dark cleft of some rock in a weary land, He lets the splendors of the outskirts of Himself pass before our gaze."

Applying God's Truth:

1. How do you tend to react when God chooses not to reveal what lies ahead for you?

2. On a scale of 1 (least) to 10 (most), how strong is your faith "in the darkness"? How could it be stronger?

3. What are some things you discovered about God during difficult times that you might not otherwise have noticed?

Day 15

Carved in Stone

Read Job 19:21–29

> *I know that my Redeemer lives, and that in the end*
> *he will stand upon the earth.*
>
> JOB 19:25

Why, in today's reading, did Job want his words to be recorded permanently (vv. 23–24)? He thought he was going to die before God would vindicate him, and he wanted people to remember how he suffered and what he said. Bildad warned him, "The memory of [a wicked man] perishes from the earth" (18:17), and Job wanted his record to remain.

At this point, Job uttered another of his statements of faith that in this book punctuates his many expressions of grief and pain. It is significant that Job would go from the depths of despair to the heights of faith and then back into the depths again. *This is often the normal experience of people experiencing great suffering.*

In spite of what some preachers say, very few people can maintain a constant high level of faith and courage in times of severe pain and trial. John Henry Jowett, at one time known as "the greatest preacher in the English-speaking world," wrote to a friend: "I wish you wouldn't think I am such a saint. You seem to imagine that I have no ups and downs, but just a level and lofty stretch of spiritual attainment with unbroken joy and equanimity. By no means! I am often perfectly wretched, and everything appears most murky" (*John Henry Jowett,* by Arthur Porritt, Hodder and Stoughton, p. 290).

Job expressed confidence that, even if he died, he would still have a Redeemer who one day would exercise judgment on the earth (v. 25). Furthermore, Job affirmed that he himself expected to live again and see his Redeemer (vv. 26–27)! It was an affirmation of faith in the resurrection of the human body.

Applying God's Truth:

1. What things do you believe to be true about God so strongly that they could be recorded permanently—"carved in stone," so to speak?

2. Are you as open about the "lows" of your spiritual life as you are the "highs"? Do you think you *should* be?

3. What are the benefits of having the confidence that you have a living Redeemer?

Day 16

Now Ear This

Read Job 20:1—21:6

Listen carefully to my words; let this be the consolation you give me.
JOB 21:2

Listen to Job's appeal to his friends that they try to understand how he feels. "If you really want to console me, just keep quiet and listen" (v. 2, author's paraphrase). The Greek philosopher Zeno said, "The reason why we have two ears and only one mouth is that we may listen the more and talk the less." The friends thought their words would encourage Job, but he said that their silence would encourage him even more (13:13).

Job pointed out that his complaint was not against people but against God. People had not caused his afflictions, and people could not take them away. If he was impatient, it was because God had not answered him (21:3–4). The longer God waited, the worse Job's situation became. "Look at me and be astonished; clap your hand over your mouth" (v. 5).

As Job contemplated what he was about to say, it stirred him to the depths (v. 6). This was no speech from "off the top of his head," for it had to do with the basic facts of life and death. If Job's friends were in his situation, they would *see* things differently and *say* things differently.

❧❧❧

Applying God's Truth:

1. Can you think of someone to whom you could minister simply by *listening?*

2. Job's friends were trying to be helpful. Why don't you think Job appreciated their words?

3. How can you remember to show more empathy the next time you are in a position to advise or console someone?

Day 17

Lifestyle Envy

Read Job 21:7–34

Their prosperity is not in their own hands,
so I stand aloof from the counsel of the wicked.
JOB 21:16

The saddest thing about the wicked is the way they leave God out of their lives and still prosper (vv. 13–15). The wicked take credit for their wealth, but Job acknowledges that everything comes from God (1:21). How, then, can Job's three friends classify him with the wicked?

We must face the disturbing fact that too many professed Christians actually admire and envy "the lifestyle of the rich and famous." In one of his books, Dr. Kenneth Chafin tells about a pastor and deacon who were visiting prospects and stopped at a beautiful suburban home. The lawn looked like it was manicured, and two expensive cars sat in the driveway. Furthermore, the pastor and deacon could see the man of the house comfortably seated in his spacious living room, watching television. Everything about the place reeked of affluence. The deacon turned to his pastor and asked, "What kind of good news do we have for this fellow?"

In more than forty years of ministry, I have performed many weddings and watched many young Christian couples get started in their shared lives. What a joy it has been to see homes where couples set the right priorities and resist the temptation to "follow the crowd" and live for material possessions. Unfortunately, some have lost their spiritual vision and succeeded in this world—without acknowledging the Lord. Alas, "they have received their reward" (Matt. 6:2, 5, 16).

Applying God's Truth:

1. Does anything ever cause you to be jealous of others? (Bigger homes? Better cars? Nicer clothes? Fatter bank books? Larger portfolios? etc.)

2. How do you deal with twinges of jealousy when they come?

3. How do you think God feels when His people succumb to jealousy of others' material possessions?

Day 18

The Slanderers of Uz

Read Job 22

Is it for your piety that he rebukes you and brings charges against you?
Is not your wickedness great? Are not your sins endless?

JOB 22:4–5

What should have been an encouraging discussion among friends had become an angry and painful debate. Instead of trying to calm things down, Eliphaz had assumed the office of prosecuting attorney and turned the debate into a trial. It was three against one as Job sat on the ash heap and listened to his friends accuse him. According to the Jewish Talmud, "The slanderous tongue kills three: the slandered, the slanderer, and him who listens to the slander." At the ash heap in Uz, there was death all around!

Eliphaz first accused Job of the sin of pride (vv. 1–3). Job was acting as though his character and conduct were important to God and beneficial to Him in some way. Eliphaz's theology centered on a distant God who was the judge of the world but not the friend of sinners (Matt. 11:19; Luke 7:34).

But Job's character and conduct *were* important to God, for *God was using Job to silence the Devil.* Neither Job nor his three friends knew God's hidden plan, but Job had faith to believe that God was achieving some purpose in his life and would one day vindicate him. Furthermore, the character and behavior of God's people *are* important to the Lord because His people bring Him either joy or sorrow (1 Thess. 4:1; Heb. 11:5; Gen. 6:5–6; Ps. 37:23). He is not a passive, distant God who does not identify with His people, but the God who delights in them as they delight in Him (Ps. 18:19; Isa. 63:9; Heb. 4:14–16).

Applying God's Truth:

1. How do you tend to react when people make false accusations against you?

2. How do you handle those times when you know you are right but are outnumbered by those who disagree with you?

3. Can you think of how any unpleasant circumstances you are currently facing might be part of God's "hidden plan"?

Day 19

The Greater the Heat, the Purer the Gold

Read Job 23—24

He knows the way that I take; when he has tested me, I will come forth as gold.
JOB 23:10

God knew where Job was—in the furnace! But it was a furnace of God's appointment, not of Job's sin, and God would use Job's affliction to purify him and make him a better man. This is not the only answer to the question, "Why do the righteous suffer?" but it is one of the best, and it can bring the sufferer great encouragement.

Scripture often uses the image of a furnace to describe God's purifying ministry through suffering (Isa. 48:10; Deut. 4:20; Ps. 66:10). The image of believers going through the furnace of persecution is also used in 1 Peter 1:6–7 and 4:12.

When God puts His own people into the furnace, He keeps His eye on the clock and His hand on the thermostat. He knows how long and how much they can bear. We may question why He does it to begin with or why He doesn't turn down the heat or even turn it off, but our questions are only evidences of unbelief. Job 23:10 is the answer: "He knows the way that I take; when he has tested me, I will come forth as gold." *Gold does not fear the fire.* The furnace can only make the gold purer and brighter.

Applying God's Truth:

1. Before today's reading, what would you have said if a friend had asked, "Why do you think good people are allowed to suffer?"

2. Do you try to avoid the heat of "God's furnace," or do you allow hard times to purify you? Give some examples.

3. Do you trust God *completely* to protect you during your "furnace experiences"? Why or why not?

Day 20

On the Fringe

Read Job 25—26

These are but the outer fringe of his works; how faint the whisper we hear of him! Who then can understand the thunder of his power?

JOB 26:14

Bildad's speech recorded in Job 25 is the shortest in the book and focuses on God's power (vv. 1–3) and justice (vv. 4–6). It is disturbing to see how Job's friends spoke so knowingly about God when, in the end, God revealed that they really didn't know what they were talking about. Too often, those who say the most about God know the least about God.

Job first rebuked Bildad for giving him no help (26:1–4). Then Job extolled the greatness of God (vv. 5–13). The three friends must have listened impatiently because they already knew the things Job was talking about, *but they hadn't drawn the right conclusion from them*. Because they saw God's handiwork in nature, they thought they knew all about God, and therefore they could explain God to Job.

Job said that just the opposite was true (v. 14). What we see of God in creation is but the fringes of His ways, and what we hear is but a whisper of His power! Knowing a few facts about the creation of God is not the same as knowing truths about the God of creation.

The fourteenth-century British spiritual writer Richard Rolle said, "He truly knows God perfectly that finds Him incomprehensible and unable to be known." The more we learn about God, the more we discover how much more there is to know! Beware of people who claim to know all about God, for their claim is proof they know neither God nor themselves.

Applying God's Truth:

1. How do you respond to people who claim to speak for God yet obviously don't reflect His love or knowledge?

2. Think of everything you *do* know about God. What percentage of His fullness do you think your knowledge would comprise?

3. What are some things you can do to (1) know God more completely and (2) better represent Him to others?

Day 21

The Beginning of Wisdom

Read Job 27—28

The fear of the Lord—that is wisdom, and to shun evil is understanding.
JOB 28:28

The first step toward true wisdom is a reverent and respectful attitude toward God, which also involves a humble attitude toward ourselves. Personal pride is the greatest barrier to spiritual wisdom. "When pride comes, then comes disgrace, but with humility comes wisdom" (Prov. 11:2).

The next step is to ask God for wisdom (James 1:5) and make diligent use of the means He gives us for securing His wisdom, especially knowing and doing the Word of God (Matt. 7:21–29). It is not enough merely to study; we must also obey what God tells us to do (John 7:17). As we walk by faith, we discover the wisdom of God in the everyday things of life. Spiritual wisdom is not abstract; it is very personal and very practical.

As we fellowship with other believers in the church and share with one another, we can learn wisdom. Reading the best books can also help us grow in wisdom and understanding. The important thing is that we focus on Christ, for He is our wisdom (1 Cor. 1:23–24) and in Him are hidden "all the treasures of wisdom and knowledge" (Col. 2:3). The better we know Christ and the more we become like Him, the more we will walk in wisdom and understand the will of the Lord. We must allow the Holy Spirit to open the eyes of our heart, so we can see God in His Word and understand more of the riches we have in Christ (Eph. 1:15–23).

Applying God's Truth:

1. In what ways is personal pride a potential barrier for your own accumulation of spiritual wisdom?

2. What are some specific situations for which you need to ask God for additional wisdom?

3. Can you think of any good *human* resources to help provide wisdom for the situations you have listed?

Day 22

Gone but Not Forgotten

Read Job 29

How I long for the months gone by, for the days when God watched over me.
JOB 29:2

Job had opened his defense by saying that he wished he had never been born (Job 3). Here he closed his defense by remembering the blessings he and his family had enjoyed prior to his crisis. This is a good reminder that we should try to see life in a balanced way. Yes, God permits us to experience difficulties and sorrows, but God also sends victories and joys. "Shall we accept good from God, and not trouble?" (2:10). Charles Haddon Spurgeon said that too many people write their blessings in the sand but engrave their sorrows in marble.

"How I long for the months gone by, for the days when God watched over me!" (29:2). When we are experiencing trials, it is natural for us to long for "the good old days"; but our longing will not change our situation. Someone has defined "the good old days" as "a combination of a bad memory and a good imagination." In Job's case, however, his memory was accurate, and "the good old days" really were good.

There is a ministry in memory if we use it properly. In days of disappointment, it is good to "remember the deeds of the LORD ... remember [his] miracles of long ago" (Ps. 77:11). But the past must be a rudder to guide us and not an anchor to hold us back. If we try to duplicate today what we experienced yesterday, we may find ourselves in a rut that robs us of maturity.

Applying God's Truth:

1. Have you ever wished you had never been born? If so, what caused your feelings?

2. What are some potential drawbacks to being nostalgic and thinking about "the good old days"?

3. How can your memory be a "ministry" to you or someone else?

Day 23

Mud Wrestling with God

Read Job 30

*In his great power God becomes like clothing to me; he binds me like the neck of
my garment. He throws me into the mud, and I am reduced to dust and ashes.*

JOB 30:18–19

Job experienced sufferings similar to those of our Lord Jesus
Christ. In the daytime, Job endured unbearable suffering; and at
night, God wrestled with him, made his clothing like a straitjacket,
and threw him in the mud. Every night, God wrestled with Job; and
Job lost.

Job prayed to God. He even stood up and cried out for deliver-
ance, but his prayers were unanswered (v. 20). Instead of God's hand
bringing help, it only attacked Job ruthlessly and tossed him about like
a feather in a storm (vv. 21–22). Job begged for his life, but death
seemed inevitable (v. 23).

Job had faithfully helped others in their need (29:12–17), but now
nobody would help him. They wouldn't weep with him or even touch
him. He was treated like a leper who might contaminate them or like
a condemned man whom God might destroy at any time. It just wasn't
wise to get too close.

Where were the people Job had helped? Surely some of them
would have wanted to show their appreciation by encouraging their
benefactor in his time of need. But nobody came to his aid. Mark
Twain wrote, "If you pick up a starving dog and make him prosperous,
he will not bite you. This is the principal difference between a dog and

a man." But according to missionary doctor Wilfred Grenfell, "The service we render for others is really the rent we pay for our room on this earth."

Applying God's Truth:

1. Has it ever seemed that God must have some kind of personal grudge against you?

2. After you help others, but they neglect to help you in return, how is your attitude toward service affected? (Do you allow the negligence of others to affect *your* ministry?)

3. Are you as honest about your feelings toward God as Job is in 30:18–23? Why or why not?

Day 24

Eli-Who?

Read Job 31—32:1

> *So these three men stopped answering Job,*
> *because he was righteous in his own eyes.*
> JOB 32:1

J ob was silent. He had ended his defense and given oath that he was not guilty of the sins he had been accused of by his friends. Job had challenged God either to vindicate him or pass sentence on him.

Job's three friends were silent, appalled that Job had dared to speak so boldly *to* God and *about* God.

God was silent. No fire came from heaven, and no voice spoke in divine wrath. The silence was God's eloquent witness to the three friends that they were wrong in what they had said both about Job and about God.

However, in the crowd around the ash heap, one person was not silent. It was Elihu, a man so unknown that his full pedigree had to be given so people could identify him (v. 2). While Elihu said some of the same things as the other speakers, his purpose was different from theirs. He was not trying to prove that Job was a sinner, but that Job's view of God was wrong. Elihu introduced a new truth into the debate: that God sends suffering, not necessarily to punish us for our sins, but to keep us from sinning (33:15–18, 19–24) and to make us better persons (36:1–15). Paul would have agreed with the first point (2 Cor. 12:7–10) and the writer of Hebrews with the second (Heb. 12:1–11).

Applying God's Truth:

1. After Job had debated his three friends and poured out his heart to God, how do you think he felt when he heard silence rather than answers?

2. How would you have felt in his place to discover that yet another person had opinions to offer—and that he was just getting started?

3. Even though Elihu was making valid observations, do you think Job was taking them to heart? Why or why not?

Day 25

Sounds and Silence

Read Job 32:2—33:33

But Elihu ... became very angry with Job for justifying himself rather than God.
JOB 32:2

Four times we are told that Elihu was angry. He was angry with the three friends for not refuting Job, and he was angry with Job for justifying himself rather than God. Job claimed that God was wrong, and the three friends couldn't prove that Job was wrong! Bildad, Zophar, and Eliphaz had given up the cause (v. 15) and were waiting for God to come and deal personally with Job (vv. 12–13). Elihu was disgusted at their failure.

"It is easy to fly into a passion—anybody can do that," wrote Aristotle. "But to be angry with the right person to the right extent and at the right time and with the right object and in the right way—that is not easy, and it is not everyone who can do it."

Elihu promised Job that God would radically alter his situation if only he would humble himself. It would be like a new birth (33:25)! He would once more enjoy prayer and fellowship with God (v. 26). If he would confess his sins and admit that God had punished him far less than he deserved (v. 27), Job would move out of the darkness into the light and gladly bear witness of God's redemption (v. 28).

Verses 31–33 suggest that Elihu wanted Job's response, but at the same time Elihu wanted Job to keep quiet! Elihu was filled to the brim with his subject and didn't want to stop talking. But Job didn't reply because he was waiting for God to speak. Job had already stated his case and thrown down the gauntlet. What Elihu thought about him or said to him made little difference to Job.

Job had taken his case to a much higher court, and when Elihu finished speaking, the Judge would appear.

Applying God's Truth:

1. Do you think anger ever affects your ministry to others? In what specific ways?

2. When was the last time you felt you were angry "with the right person to the right extent and at the right time and with the right object and in the right way"?

3. Is it easy for you to ignore someone who is very angry? What do you think Job's lack of response to Elihu indicated about his mind-set?

Day 26

Defending God

Read Job 34—35

> *Listen to me, you men of understanding. Far be it from*
> *God to do evil, from the Almighty to do wrong.*
>
> JOB 34:10

Theology ("the science of God") used to be called "the queen of sciences" because it deals with the most important knowledge we can have: the knowledge of God. Theology is a necessary science, but it is also a difficult science; for it is our attempt to know the Unknowable (Rom. 11:33–36). God has revealed Himself in creation, in providence, in His Word, and supremely in His Son; but our understanding of what God has revealed may not always be clear.

"The essence of idolatry," wrote A. W. Tozer, "is the entertainment of thoughts about God that are unworthy of Him" (*The Knowledge of the Holy,* Harper and Row, p. 11). So, whoever attempts to explain and defend the Almighty must have the humble heart of a worshipper; for "knowledge puffs up, but love builds up" (1 Cor. 8:1).

As we read Elihu's speeches, we get the impression that he was not growing; he was swelling. We also get the impression that his listeners' minds were wandering, because he kept exhorting them to listen carefully (Job 33:1, 31, 33; 34:2, 10, 16).

Yet Elihu emphasized that God is sovereign, and the book of Job magnifies the sovereignty of God. From the very first chapter, it is obvious that God is in control; for even Satan is told what he can and cannot do. During the debate, it appears that God is absent, but He is aware of how Job feels and what Job and his friends are saying. Elihu was right on target: God is sovereign and cannot do wrong.

Applying God's Truth:

1. What are some questions of theology that have come up in your interactions with skeptics or people of other faiths?

2. Do you know religious people who are "all theory and no practicality"? How might people avoid such a problem?

3. Even though Elihu was "right on target," do you think Job benefited from his words? Why or why not?

Day 27

A Helpful, but Overlooked, Ministry

Read Job 36—37

> *How great is God—beyond our understanding!*
> *The number of his years is past finding out.*
>
> JOB 36:26

Elihu urged Job to catch a new vision of the greatness of God and start praising Him (vv. 22–25). God wants to teach us through our sufferings (v. 22), and one evidence that we are learning our lessons is that we praise and thank Him, even for trials. "Glorify him for his mighty works for which he is so famous" (v. 24 TLB). "Praise changes things" just as much as "prayer changes things."

With all his verbosity and lack of humility, Elihu did say some good things that Job needed to hear. Elihu's use of rhetorical questions in 37:14–18 prepared Job for the series of questions Jehovah would ask him in Job 38—41. Unlike the three friends, Elihu assessed Job's problem accurately: Job's *actions* may have been right—he was not the sinner his three friends described him to be—but his *attitudes* were wrong. He was not the "saint" Job saw himself to be. Job was slowly moving toward a defiant, self-righteous attitude that was not at all healthy. It was this "know-it-all" attitude that God exposed and destroyed when He appeared to Job and questioned him.

So, even though God said nothing about Elihu, the man did have a helpful ministry to Job. Unfortunately, Job wouldn't accept it.

Applying God's Truth:

1. What are some things you will always be able to praise God for—even when everything seems to be going wrong?

2. Can you think of anyone who has tried—sincerely—to minister to you in some way, but you have ignored that person's efforts? What can you do to begin to show appreciation?

3. What are some good actions you have performed lately in which your attitudes weren't quite as good as they should have been?

Day 28

God Responds

Read Job 38—41

Then the LORD answered Job out of the storm.
JOB 38:1

W̶e prefer that God speak to us in the sunshine, but sometimes He must speak out of the storm. Experiencing this majestic demonstration of God's power made Job very susceptible to the message God had for him. God's address to Job centered on His works in nature and consisted of seventy-seven questions interspersed with divine commentary relating to the questions. The whole purpose of this interrogation was to make Job realize his own inadequacy and inability to meet God as an equal and defend his cause.

"Summon me and I will answer," Job had challenged God, "or let me speak, and you reply" (13:22). God had now responded to Job's challenge.

Job was sure that his speeches had been filled with wisdom and knowledge, but God's first question put an end to that delusion: "Who is this that darkens my counsel with words without knowledge?" (38:2). *The Living Bible* paraphrases it, "Why are you using your ignorance to deny my providence?" God didn't question Job's integrity or sincerity; He only questioned Job's ability to explain the ways of God in the world. Job had spoken the truth about God (42:7), but his speeches had lacked humility. Job thought he knew about God, but he didn't realize how much he *didn't* know about God. Knowledge of our own ignorance is the first step toward true wisdom.

Applying God's Truth:

1. When was the last time God "spoke" to you through His creation?

2. Job and his friends had debated God's will for a long time. How do you suppose they felt when God eventually began to speak for Himself?

3. If "knowledge of our own ignorance is the first step toward true wisdom," have you taken a giant step, a medium step, or a baby step? Explain.

Day 29

From Sinner to Servant

Read Job 42:1–6

Then Job replied to the LORD: "I know that you can do all things....
Therefore I despise myself and repent in dust and ashes."
JOB 42:1–2, 6

Job knew he was beaten. There was no way he could argue his case
with God. Quoting God's very words (vv. 3–4), Job humbled himself before the Lord and acknowledged His power and justice in exe-
cuting His plans (v. 2). Then Job admitted that his words had been
wrong and that he had spoken about things he didn't understand (v.
3). Job withdrew his accusations that God was unjust and treating him
unfairly. He realized that whatever God does is right and that he must
accept it by faith.

Job told God, "I can't answer Your questions! All I can do is confess my pride, humble myself, and repent." Until now, Job's
knowledge of God had been indirect and impersonal, but that was
changed. Job had met God personally and seen himself to be but
"dust and ashes."

"The door of repentance opens into the hall of joy," said Charles
Haddon Spurgeon, and it was true for Job. In the climax of the book,
Job the sinner became Job the servant of God. How did Job serve
God? By enduring suffering and not cursing God and thereby silenc-
ing the Devil! Suffering in the will of God is a ministry God gives to a
chosen few.

Applying God's Truth:

1. When you realize you are wrong about something, how quick are you to repent?

2. In terms of percentages, how much of your own transformation from sinner to servant of God do you think is complete?

3. Do you know any individuals for whom you think suffering is a "ministry"? What can you do to encourage such people?

Day 30

God as Author

Read Job 42:7–17

> *After Job had prayed for his friends, the* LORD *made him prosperous
> again and gave him twice as much as he had before.*
>
> JOB 42:10

Job ended up with twice as much as he had before. He had twenty
children, ten with God and ten in his home (vv. 13–15). (He and his
wife were also reunited.) Friends and relatives brought money for a
restoration fund (v. 11), which Job must have used for purchasing
breeders, and eventually, Job had twice as much livestock as before (v.
12). He was once again a wealthy man.

But we must not misinterpret this final chapter and conclude that
every trial will end with all problems solved, all hard feelings forgiven,
and everybody living "happily ever after." It just doesn't always happen that way! This chapter assures us that, no matter what happens to
us, *God always writes the last chapter*. Therefore, we don't have to be
afraid. We can trust God to do what is right, no matter how painful
our situation may be.

But Job's greatest blessing was not the regaining of his health and
wealth or the rebuilding of his family and circle of friends. His greatest blessing was *knowing God better and understanding His working
in a deeper way*. "In the whole story of Job," wrote G. Campbell
Morgan, "we see the patience of God and endurance of man. When
these act in fellowship, the issue is certain. It is that of the coming

forth from the fire as gold, that of receiving the crown of life" (*The Answers of Jesus to Job*, Baker, p. 117).

No matter what God permits to come into our lives, He always has His "afterward." He writes the last chapter—and that makes it all worthwhile.

Applying God's Truth:

1. Would you say that Job's story had a happy ending? Why or why not?

2. Do you think you can learn to know God better without going through the depth of suffering that Job experienced? Explain.

3. Think back to the things you were suffering as you began reading through Job. How, if at all, has your perspective changed in regard to your problems?

Wholeness

Thirty Daily Readings from the Book of Colossians

Today we live in a world that lacks integrity, and one word describes the lives and experiences of many people: "fragmented."

Some people's lives are in pieces because they can't handle the pressures that come their way. Problems arise, and these people fall apart. Other people are fragmented because they don't know who they are, and they lack a foundation on which to build their lives. Still others aren't whole because they are trying to please too many people and reach too many goals, not all of them worthy goals.

In other words, some people are blown apart, some are pulled apart, and some are just quietly falling apart.

Which are you?

Fragmented people are unhappy people. They try to keep up a bold front, but even that pretense becomes another part of their disintegrated lives. Pretending only makes thing worse.

Paul's letter to the Christians in Colosse explains that Jesus Christ is holding this universe together and *can hold our lives together if we will trust Him.* "In him all things hold together" (1:17) is one of the main messages of this important letter, a message that can make a difference in your life today.

But let me give a word of warning: This isn't a theological ABC book for amateurs. It is a book of solid theology for people who are serious about putting their lives together and making them amount to something in the will of God. It is for Christians who will read and meditate and think. If you take this book seriously, Jesus Christ will help you integrate your life, and the God who runs the universe will help manage your life and keep it together.

You will move from *fragmentation* to *integration* as Jesus Christ exercises His lordship and power in your daily life.

You will be a whole person in a broken world, and you will help others to find this wholeness through faith in Jesus Christ.

Day 1

Good Beginnings

Read Colossians 1:1–2

> *To the holy and faithful brothers in Christ at Colosse:*
> *Grace and peace to you from God our Father.*
>
> COLOSSIANS 1:2

Colosse probably would never have been mentioned in the New Testament had it not been for the church there. The city is never named in the book of Acts because Paul did not start the Colossian church, nor did he ever visit it. Paul had *heard* of their faith (Col. 1:4, 9), but he had never seen these believers personally (2:1). Here was a church of unknown people, in a small town, receiving an inspired letter from the great apostle Paul!

How did the Colossian church begin? It was the outgrowth of Paul's three-year ministry in Ephesus (Acts 19; 20:17–38). So effective was the witness of the church at Ephesus that "all the Jews and Greeks who lived in the province of Asia heard the word of the Lord" (19:10).

There is a good lesson for us here: God does not always need an apostle, or a "full-time Christian worker," to get a ministry established. Nor does He need elaborate buildings and extensive organizations. Here laypeople were used by God to start ministries. It is God's plan that the Christians in the large urban areas, like Ephesus, reach out into the smaller towns and share the gospel. Is your church helping to evangelize "small-town" mission fields?

Applying God's Truth:

1. On a scale of 1 (least) to 10 (most), how sensitive do you think your church is in recognizing the spiritual needs of its surrounding communities?

2. On the same scale, how sensitive are you personally to the needs of others around you?

3. What is one thing you can do this week to increase your own or your church's awareness of surrounding needs?

Day 2

A Note of Encouragement

Read Colossians 1:3–4

> *We always thank God, the Father of our Lord Jesus Christ,*
> *when we pray for you, because we have heard of your faith in*
> *Christ Jesus and of the love you have for all the saints.*
>
> COLOSSIANS 1:3–4

The famous Scottish preacher Alexander Whyte was known as an appreciator. He loved to write postcards to people, thanking them for some kindness or blessing they had brought to his life. Those messages often brought a touch of encouragement to a heart just when it was needed most. Appreciation is great medicine for the soul.

The apostle Paul was a great encourager, and this epistle is a good example of the grace of thanksgiving. In this section he gave thanks for what Christ had done in the lives of the Colossian Christians. But he also mentioned thanksgiving in five other places in this letter. When we recall that Paul wrote this letter in prison, his attitude of thanksgiving is even more wonderful.

Like Paul, we should be grateful for what God is doing in the lives of others. As Christians, we are all members of one body (Rom. 12:5). If one member of the body is strengthened, this helps to strengthen the entire body (1 Cor. 12:12–26). If one church experiences a revival touch from God, it will help all the churches.

Applying God's Truth:

1. When other people receive praise or recognition, are you usually glad for them or a bit jealous? Why?

2. How do you tend to respond when you do something nice for someone who shows no appreciation?

3. Can you think of people for whom you should show appreciation? If so, what are some specific ways to do so?

Day 3

The Gospel Truth

Read Colossians 1:5–6

The faith and love that spring from the hope that is stored up
for you in heaven and that you have already heard about
in the word of truth, the gospel that has come to you.

Colossians 1:5–6

There are many messages and ideas that can be called true, but only God's Word can be called truth. Satan is a liar (John 8:44); to believe his lies is to be led astray into death. Jesus is the Truth (John 14:6); when we trust Him, we experience life (John 10:10). Many people have tried to destroy God's truth, but they have failed. The Word of Truth still stands!

Everybody has faith in something. But faith is only as good as the object in which people put their trust. Ignorant tribal pagans worshipped gods of stone; modern educated city pagans worship money or possessions or status. In both cases, faith is empty. True Christian believers have faith in Jesus Christ, and that faith is based on the Word of Truth. Any other kind of faith is nothing but superstition—it cannot save.

John Selden (1584–1654) was a leading historian and legal authority in England. He had a library of eight thousand volumes and was recognized for his learning. When he was dying, he said to Archbishop James Ussher: "I have surveyed most of the learning that is among the sons of men, and my study is filled with books and manuscripts on various subjects. But at present, I cannot recollect any passage out of all my books and papers whereon I can rest my soul, save this from the sacred Scriptures: 'The grace of God that bringeth salvation hath appeared to all men'" (Titus 2:11 KJV).

Applying God's Truth:

1. What are some of the subtle lies you have heard others promote in regard to Christianity?

2. In what things do you tend to put your faith? To what extent do these things affect your faith in Christ?

3. What is one verse or passage from God's truth that might help you keep your faith strong today?

Day 4

Seed Power

Read Colossians 1:6–8

All over the world this gospel is bearing fruit and growing,
just as it has been doing among you since the day you heard
it and understood God's grace in all its truth.

Colossians 1:6

The Word of God is seed (Luke 8:11). This means the Word has life in it. When it is planted in the heart, it can produce fruit.

Near King's Cross station in London, England, there is a cemetery containing a unique grave, that of the agnostic Lady Ann Grimston. She is buried in a marble tomb, marked by a marble slab. Before she died, she said sarcastically to a friend, "I shall live again as surely as a tree will grow from my body."

An unbeliever, Lady Ann Grimston did not believe that there was life after death. However, *a tree did grow from her grave!* A tiny seed took root, and as it grew, it cracked the marble and even tore the metal railing out of the ground! There is life and power in a seed, and there is life and power in the Word of God.

When God's Word is planted and cultivated, it produces fruit. Faith, hope, and love are among the firstfruits in the spiritual harvest (1 Cor. 13:13). These spiritual graces are among the evidences that we have truly been born again.

Applying God's Truth:

1. What are you reaping as a result of God's Word sown in your heart?

2. What do you do to help sow the Word in the hearts of others?

3. Based on the amount of growth of God's Word in your life, would you describe yourself as (a) still a seed, (b) a sprout, (c) a sapling, (d) a growing tree, or (e) a mighty oak?

Day 5

Complete!

Read Colossians 1:9

*Since the day we heard about you, we have not stopped praying
for you and asking God to fill you with the knowledge of his
will through all spiritual wisdom and understanding.*

COLOSSIANS 1:9

When we are born into God's family by faith in Jesus Christ, we are born with all we need for growth and maturity. This is the theme of Colossians: "You have been given fullness in Christ" (2:10). No other experience is needed than the new birth. "Do not look for something new," Paul warned the church. "Continue to grow in that which you received at the beginning" (author's paraphrase).

Each of us needs to have the "knowledge of his will." The Greek word translated "knowledge" in this verse carries the meaning of "full knowledge." There is always more to learn about God and His will for our lives. As Christians we should never dare to say that we have "arrived" and need to learn nothing more. Like the college freshman who handed in a ten-page report on "The History of the Universe," we would only declare our ignorance.

The will of God is an important part of a successful Christian life. God wants us to *know* His will and *understand* it. God is not a distant dictator who issues orders and never explains. Because we are His friends (James 2:23; John 15:13–15), we can know what He is doing and why He is doing it. As we study His Word and pray, we discover new and exciting truths about God's will for us as His people.

Applying God's Truth:

1. If your sense of feeling complete in Jesus were represented by a gasoline gauge on a car, would your reading be "Full," "Empty," or somewhere in between?

2. If you believe you are complete in Christ (Col. 2:10 KJV) but don't *feel* complete, what should you do?

3. What steps can you take in order to better know and understand God's will for your life by, say, this time next week?

Day 6

Walking and Working

Read Colossians 1:10

*We pray this in order that you may live a life worthy of
the Lord and may please him in every way.*

COLOSSIANS 1:10

The false teachers in Colosse attracted people through their offer of "spiritual knowledge," but they did not relate this knowledge to life. In the Christian life, knowledge and obedience go together. There is no separation between *learning* and *living*. The wisdom about which Paul prayed was not simply a head knowledge of deep spiritual truths. True spiritual wisdom must affect the daily life. Wisdom and practical intelligence must go together.

In my pastoral ministry, I have met people who have become intoxicated with "studying the deeper truths of the Bible." Usually they have been given a book or introduced to some teacher's tapes. Before long, they get so smart they become dumb! All biblical truths are practical, not theoretical. If we are growing in knowledge, we should also be growing in grace.

Three words summarize the practicality of the Christian life: *wisdom, walk,* and *work*. The sequence is important: first, wisdom; then walk; then work. We cannot work for God unless we are walking with Him, but we cannot walk with Him if we are ignorant of His will. If we spend time daily in the Word and prayer, we will know God's will and be able to walk with Him and work for Him.

Applying God's Truth:

1. On a scale where 1 = "Knowledge of Scripture and No Application," 10 = "Lots of 'Christian' Activity with No Real Depth," and 5 = "An Ideal Balance of Knowledge and Action," where would you be?

2. What are you doing to improve your walk with God?

3. What are you doing to improve your work for Him?

Day 7

Four Factors

Read Colossians 1:11–14

Bearing fruit in every good work, growing in the knowledge of God, being strengthened with all power … and joyfully giving thanks to the Father.
COLOSSIANS 1:10–12

Wisdom and conduct should always be related to moral character. One of the great problems in our evangelical world today is the emphasis on "spiritual knowledge" and "Christian service," without connecting these important matters to personal character.

For example, some teachers and preachers claim to have God's wisdom—yet they lack love and kindness and the other basic qualities that make the Christian life beautiful and distinctive. Even some "soul-winning Christians" are so busy serving God that they cannot take time to check facts, so they publish lies about other Christians. For some months, I read a certain religious publication. But when I discovered that it had no "Letters to the Editor" column (except for praise) and that it had never published a correction or apologized for an error, I stopped reading the magazine.

Knowledge, conduct, service, and character must always go together. We know God's will so that we can obey it; and, in obeying it, we serve Him and grow in Christian character. While none of us is perfectly balanced in these four factors, we ought to strive for that balance.

Applying God's Truth:

1. If you never told other people you were a Christian, how long do you think it would take them to notice? Why?

2. Can you take constructive criticism as well as you receive praise? Why or why not?

3. If you made a pie chart to graphically represent the characteristics of knowledge, conduct, service, and character in your life, what would the individual percentages be? (The total should be 100 percent.)

Day 8

All You Need

Read Colossians 1:15

[Jesus] is the image of the invisible God, the firstborn over all creation.
COLOSSIANS 1:15

Paul's main theme in Colossians is the preeminence of Jesus Christ (v. 18 KJV). There is no need for us to worry about angelic mediators or spiritual emanations. God sent His Son to die for us! Every person who believes on Jesus Christ is saved (John 3:36) and is a part of His body, the church, of which He is the Head (Col. 1:18). We are united to Christ in a wonderful, living relationship!

While in an airport waiting for my plane to be called, I was approached by a young man who wanted to sell me a book. One look at the garish cover told me the book was filled with Oriental myths and philosophies.

"I have a book here that meets all my needs," I told the young man, and I reached into my briefcase and took out my Bible.

"Oh, we aren't against the Bible!" he assured me. "It's just that we have something more, and it makes our faith even better."

"Nobody can give me more than Jesus Christ has already given me," I replied. Sad to say, there are many Christians who actually believe that some person, religious system, or discipline can add something to their spiritual experience. But they already have everything they will ever need in the person and work of Jesus Christ.

Applying God's Truth:

1. During the past twenty-four hours, what are some of the things you have seen other people put before Christ?

2. What are some things you tend (or have tended) to let interfere with your relationship with Jesus?

3. How do people you know sometimes try to add to the gospel? Why do you think they do so?

Day 9

Holding It Together

Read Colossians 1:16–17

> *[Jesus] is before all things, and in him all things hold together.*
> COLOSSIANS 1:17

Aguide took a group of people through an atomic laboratory and explained how all matter was composed of rapidly moving particles. The tourists studied models of molecules and were amazed to learn that matter is made up primarily of space. During the question period, one visitor asked, "If this is the way matter works, what holds it all together?" For that, the guide had no answer.

But the Christian has an answer: Jesus Christ! Because "he is before all things," He can hold all things together. This is another affirmation that Jesus Christ is God. Only God existed before all of creation (Gen. 1:1–2), and only God can make creation cohere. To make Jesus Christ less than God is to dethrone Him.

It used to bother me to sing the familiar song "This Is My Father's World." I thought Satan and sin were in control of this world. I have since changed my mind, and now I sing the song with joy and victory. Jesus Christ made all things (John 1:1–3), He controls all things, and by Him all things hold together. Indeed this is my Father's world!

Applying God's Truth:

1. If you increasingly believe that Jesus holds all things together,

what are some situations you are currently facing in which you should trust Him more?

2. Have you yielded every area of your life to God's wise control? If not, what else do you need to trust Him to handle?

3. Believing that Jesus is before all things, what are some potentially stressful things you expect to face in the future that you should leave in His hands?

Day 10

The Greatest Attraction

Read Colossians 1:18–20

And he is the head of the body, the church; he is the beginning and the firstborn
from among the dead, so that in everything he might have the supremacy.
COLOSSIANS 1:18

In 1893, the World's Columbian Exposition was held in Chicago, and more than twenty-one million people visited the exhibits. Among the features was a "World Parliament of Religions," with representatives of the world's religions meeting to share their "best points" and perhaps come up with a new religion for the world.

Evangelist D. L. Moody saw this as a great opportunity for evangelism. He used churches, rented theaters, and even rented a circus tent (when the show was not on) to present the gospel of Jesus Christ. His friends wanted Moody to attack the "Parliament of Religions," but he refused. "I am going to make Jesus Christ so attractive," he said, "that men will turn to Him." Moody knew that Jesus Christ was the preeminent Savior, not just one of many "religious leaders" of history.

But the false teachers of Colosse could never give Jesus Christ His rightful place of preeminence (see Col. 1:18 KJV); for, according to their philosophy, Jesus Christ was only one of the many "emanations" from God. He was not the only way to God; rather, He was but one rung on the ladder! But Jesus said, "I am the way and the truth and the life. No one comes to the Father except through me" (John 14:6). It has well been said, "If Jesus Christ is not Lord of all, He cannot be Lord at all."

Applying God's Truth:

1. How do you usually respond when confronted by people of other religions?

2. What do cults and other religions promise in order to recruit followers? How might you respond to their claims based on Colossians 1:18?

3. What are three specific things you can do this week to try to "make Jesus [more] attractive" to others?

Day 11

How Firm Your Foundation?

Read Colossians 1:21–23

> *Now [God] has reconciled you by Christ's physical body*
> *through death to present you holy in his sight, without blemish*
> *and free from accusation—if you continue in your faith, established*
> *and firm, not moved from the hope held out in the gospel.*
>
> COLOSSIANS 1:22–23

Paul's statement to the Colossians seems to cast a shadow on the assurance of our future glory (v. 13). Is it possible for us believers to lose our salvation? No, the *if* clause in verse 23 does not suggest doubt or lay down a condition by which we "continue in [our] faith."

Paul used an architectural image in this verse—a house, firmly set on the foundation. The town of Colosse was located in a region known for earthquakes, and the Greek word translated "moved from" can mean "earthquake stricken." Paul was saying, "If you are truly saved and built on the solid foundation, Jesus Christ, then you will continue in the faith and nothing will move you. You have heard the gospel and trusted Jesus Christ, and He has saved you."

In other words, we are not saved by continuing in the faith. But we continue in the faith and thus prove that we are saved. It behooves each of us as professing Christians to test our own faith and examine our own heart to be sure we are a child of God (2 Cor. 13:5).

❧

Applying God's Truth:

1. What tends to make Christians question their assurance of salvation?

2. What are some of the "earthquakes" you have faced that threatened to shake your spiritual foundation?

3. What can you learn from these verses that will help you face future "earthquakes"?

Day 12

Everybody In!

Read Colossians 1:24–27

To them God has chosen to make known among the Gentiles the glorious riches of this mystery, which is Christ in you, the hope of glory.

<small>COLOSSIANS 1:27</small>

God has initiated a new program—His *mystery*—that was not explained by the Old Testament prophets. The mystery is that today God is uniting Jews and Gentiles in the church (Eph. 3:2–6). Imagine what this message meant to the Gentiles. They were no longer excluded from the glory and riches of God's grace! During the Old Testament dispensation, a Gentile had to become a Jewish proselyte in order to share in the blessings of Israel. But in the new dispensation, Jews and Gentiles alike are saved by faith in Jesus Christ (Rom. 10:12–13).

We who have grown up in somewhat Christian surroundings have a tendency to take all this for granted. But think of the excitement this message must have generated in a church composed of new believers who had no background in the church.

I was privileged to minister in Africa for three weeks, and there I was introduced to some of the finest Christians I have ever met. I taught the Word to more than five hundred national pastors in Kenya for almost a week, and each service was a challenge and blessing to me. Many of the pastors still had the marks of paganism and idolatry on their bodies, yet their faces were aglow with the joy of the Lord. I went to Africa to minister to them, but they ministered to me! They reminded me not to take for granted the glorious riches I have in Jesus Christ.

Applying God's Truth:

1. Do you ever feel "left out" at church or in other Christian groups? In what ways?

2. Put yourself in the place of a Gentile believer hearing Paul's words for the first time. Describe your feelings.

3. What are some ways you can minister to people who usually minister to you?

Day 13

Prayer at Work

Read Colossians 1:28–29

We proclaim him, admonishing and teaching everyone with all wisdom,
so that we may present everyone perfect in Christ. To this end I labor,
struggling with all his energy, which so powerfully works in me.

COLOSSIANS 1:28–29

A more literal translation of the first part of Colossians 1:29 is "For this I labor to the point of exhaustion, agonizing." What a picture of prayer! So much of our praying is calm and comfortable, and yet Paul exerted his spiritual muscles the way a Greek runner would exert himself in the Olympic Games.

This does not mean that our prayers are more effective if we exert all kinds of fleshly energy. Nor does it mean that we must "wrestle with God" and wear Him out before He will meet our needs. Paul described a *spiritual* striving: It was God's power at work in his life.

Prayer is not our trying to change God's mind. It is learning what is the mind of God and asking accordingly (1 John 5:14–15). The Holy Spirit constantly intercedes for us even though we do not hear His voice (Rom. 8:26–27). He knows the Father's will, and He helps us pray in that will.

There are times when we simply do not feel like praying—and that is when we must pray the most! The Spirit gives us divine energy for prayer, in spite of the way we feel. The resurrection power of Jesus Christ is made available to us.

Applying God's Truth:

1. As a prayer, would you say you are more like an Olympic marathoner, a long-distance runner, an occasional sprinter, or a couch potato?

2. In what ways do you motivate yourself to pray when you don't feel like it?

3. When could you set aside time and "labor to the point of exhaustion" in prayer?

Day 14

Fighting the Wolves

Read Colossians 2:1–7

*Just as you received Christ Jesus as Lord, continue to live in him,
rooted and built up in him, strengthened in the faith as you
were taught, and overflowing with thankfulness.*

COLOSSIANS 2:6–7

I recall a story about a pastor who was concerned about some unsavory businesses that had opened near a school. His protests finally led to a court case, and the defense attorney did all he could to embarrass the gospel minister.

"Are you not a pastor?" the lawyer asked. "And doesn't the word 'pastor' mean 'shepherd'?" To this definition the minister agreed.

"Well, if you are a shepherd, why aren't you out taking care of the sheep?"

"Because today I'm fighting the wolves!" was the pastor's quick reply, and a good answer it was.

Knowing that there were enemies already attacking the church in Colosse, Paul offered encouragement. By heeding his admonitions, the Colossians would overcome their enemies.

In the Christian life, we never stand still: We either go forward or gradually slip backward. "Let us … go on to maturity!" is the call we must obey (Heb. 6:1). Christians who are not making spiritual progress are an open target for the Enemy to attack and destroy (1 Peter 5:8–9).

Applying God's Truth:

1. What are some of the current "wolves" in your life?

2. In your spiritual life, would you say you have been gradually slipping backward, making occasional progress, or making regular progress? How could you "pick up the pace"?

3. As you go forward, are you "overflowing with thankfulness"? If not, what are some things you could try?

Day 15

Sharing the Fullness

Read Colossians 2:8–15

> *In Christ all the fullness of the Deity lives in bodily form, and you have been given fullness in Christ, who is the head over every power and authority.*
> Colossians 2:9–10

When Jesus Christ ascended to heaven, He went in a human body (Acts 1:1–11). It was a glorified body, to be sure, but it was real. After His resurrection, our Lord was careful to assure His disciples that He was the same person in the same body; He was not a ghost or a spirit (John 20:19–29). There is a glorified Man in heaven! The God-man, Jesus Christ, embodies the fullness of God!

Now, the remarkable thing is this: *Every believer shares that fullness!* "You have been given fullness in Christ" (Col. 2:10). The tense of the Greek verb indicates that this fullness is a permanent experience. Dr. Kenneth Wuest's very literal *Expanded Translation* reads, "And you are in Him, having been completely filled full with the present result that you are in a state of fullness."

When we are born again into the family of God, we are born complete in Christ. Our spiritual growth is not by *addition,* but by *nutrition.* We grow from the inside out. Nothing needs to be added to Christ because He already is the very fullness of God. As we draw on Christ's fullness, we are "filled to the measure of all the fullness of God" (Eph. 3:19). What more do we need?

Applying God's Truth:

1. What does it mean to you that Jesus ascended to heaven in a real body?

2. If someone saw you on an average day, do you think that person could tell that "you have been given fullness in Christ"? Why or why not?

3. Since nothing needs to be added to what you are, how can you continue to mature as a Christian?

Day 16

Playing by the Rules

Read Colossians 2:16–19

> *Do not let anyone who delights in false humility and the worship of*
> *angels disqualify you for the prize. Such a person goes into great detail about*
> *what he has seen, and his unspiritual mind puffs him up with idle notions.*
>
> COLOSSIANS 2:18

The word translated "disqualify" means "to declare unworthy of a prize." It is an athletic term: The umpire disqualifies contestants who do not obey the rules. The contestants do not cease to be citizens of the land, but they forfeit the honor of winning a prize. Christians who fail to obey God's directions do not lose their salvation. But they do lose the approval of the Lord and the rewards He has promised to those who are faithful (1 Cor. 3:8).

It is a gracious act of God that He has promised rewards to those who serve Him. Certainly He does not owe us anything! We ought to be so grateful that He has saved us from judgment that we would serve Him whether or not we received a reward. Most of God's servants probably obey Him out of love and devotion and never think about rewards. Just as there are degrees of punishment in hell (Matt. 23:15), so there will be degrees of glory in heaven—even though all believers will be like Christ in their glorified bodies (1 John 3:2).

The old Puritan Thomas Watson said it perfectly: "Though every vessel of mercy shall be full [in heaven], yet one may hold more than another."

Applying God's Truth:

1. How do you feel when you are in a competition where lots of people are cheating? How does this situation apply to today's verse?

2. Which of God's rules do you tend to break or "stretch" from time to time?

3. In addition to eternal rewards you may miss if you are misled by others in regard to God's truth, what could you be missing out on now?

Day 17

Too Much Self-Denial

Read Colossians 2:20–23

> *Since you died with Christ to the basic principles of this world, why,*
> *as though you still belonged to it, do you submit to its rules:*
> *"Do not handle! Do not taste! Do not touch!"?*
>
> COLOSSIANS 2:20–21

Paul first condemned legalism and mysticism; next he attacked and condemned *asceticism*. Ascetics practice rigorous self-denial and even self-mortification in order to become more spiritual. Ascetic practices were popular during the Middle Ages: wearing hair shirts next to the skin, sleeping on hard beds, whipping oneself, not speaking for days (maybe years), going without food or sleep, etc.

There is a definitely a relationship between legalism and asceticism, for ascetics often subject themselves to rules and regulations. As Christians, we admit that physical discipline is needed in our lives. Many of us eat too much and are overweight. Some of us drink too much coffee or cola drinks and are nervous and upset. We believe that our bodies are temples of the Holy Spirit (1 Cor. 6:19), yet sometimes we do not care for our bodies as we should. There is a place in our Christian lives for proper care of our bodies.

But ascetics hope to sanctify the soul by discipline of the body, and it is this heresy that Paul attacked. Just as days and diets have no sanctifying value, neither does fleshly discipline (Col. 2:22–23).

Applying God's Truth:

1. While we may not wear hair shirts or whip ourselves, can you think of any somewhat ascetic practices of certain Christians today?

2. What do you think are the benefits of incorporating physical disciplines into spiritual maturity?

3. What are the potential drawbacks?

Day 18

Looking Up

Read Colossians 3:1–2

> *Since, then, you have been raised with Christ, set your*
> *hearts on things above, where Christ is seated at the right hand*
> *of God. Set your minds on things above, not on earthly things.*
>
> COLOSSIANS 3:1–2

How do we set our hearts on "things above"? The secret is found in a literal translation of verse 2: "Habitually set your mind—your attention—on things above, not on things on the earth." Our feet must be on earth, but our minds must be in heaven. This is not to suggest that (as D. L. Moody used to say) we become "so heavenly minded that we are no earthly good." It means that the practical everyday affairs of life get their direction from Christ in heaven. It means further that we look at earth from heaven's point of view.

While attending a convention in Washington, D.C., I watched a Senate committee hearing on television. I believe they were considering a new ambassador to the United Nations. The late Senator Hubert Humphrey was making a comment as I turned on the television set: "You must remember that in politics, how you stand depends on where you sit." He was referring, of course, to the political party seating arrangement in the Senate, but I immediately applied it to our position in Christ. How we stand—and walk—depends on where we sit, *and we are seated with Christ in the heavenlies!* (Eph. 2:6).

Applying God's Truth:

1. What are three things that are currently interfering with your ability to "seek those things which are above" (Col. 3:1 KJV)?

2. How can you be "heavenly minded" more frequently and still be "earthly good"?

3. Envision yourself seated with Christ right now. What would you want to ask or tell Him?

Day 19

A Matter of Life and Death

Read Colossians 3:3–4

For you died, and your life is now hidden with Christ in God. When Christ, who is your life, appears, then you also will appear with him in glory.

<small>COLOSSIANS 3:3–4</small>

Christ not only died *for* us (substitution), but we died *with* Him (identification). Christ not only died *for* sin, bearing its penalty; He also died *unto* sin, breaking its power. Because we are "in Christ" through the work of the Holy Spirit (1 Cor. 12:13), we died with Christ. This means that we can have victory over the old sin nature that wants to control us.

Someone has said, "Life is what you are alive to." A child may come alive when you talk about a baseball game or an ice-cream cone. A teenager may come alive when you mention cars or dates. Paul wrote, "For to me, to live is Christ" (Phil. 1:21). Christ was Paul's life, and he was alive to anything that related to Christ. So should it be with every believer.

Years ago I heard a story about two sisters who enjoyed attending dances and wild parties. Then they were converted and found new life in Christ. They received an invitation to a party and sent their RSVP in these words: "We regret that we cannot attend because we recently died."

Applying God's Truth:

1. How do you feel when you think of how Christ died for you?

2. Do you feel the same way when you think of how you died with Him? Explain.

3. What makes you "come alive"? Do any of these things interfere with your being able to exclaim, "For to me, to live is Christ"?

Day 20

Idol Time

Read Colossians 3:5–11

Put to death, therefore, whatever belongs to your earthly nature: sexual immorality, impurity, lust, evil desires and greed, which is idolatry.

COLOSSIANS 3:5

Greed (or covetousness in the King James Version) is the sin of always wanting more, whether it be more things or more pleasures. Covetous people are never satisfied with what they have, and they are usually envious of what others have. This is idolatry, for covetousness puts things in the place of God. "You shall not covet" is the last of the Ten Commandments (Ex. 20:17). Yet this sin can make us break all of the other nine! Greedy people will dishonor God, take God's name in vain, lie, steal, and commit every other sin in order to satisfy their sinful desires.

Do believers in local churches commit such sins? Unfortunately, they sometimes do. Each of the New Testament epistles sent to local churches mentions these sins and warns against them.

I am reminded of a pastor who preached a series of sermons against the sins of the saints. A member of his congregation challenged him one day and said that it would be better if the pastor preached those messages to the lost. "After all," said the church member, "sin in the lives of Christians is different from sin in the lives of other people."

"Yes," replied the pastor, "it's *worse!*"

Applying God's Truth:

1. On a scale of 1 (least) to 10 (most), how covetous (greedy) would you say you are?

2. In your own experiences, what are some additional sins you have witnessed among people who are basically greedy?

3. What things do you do to prevent covetousness from getting out of control and hindering your spiritual maturity?

Day 21

An Exclusive Relationship

Read Colossians 3:12–14

> *As God's chosen people, holy and dearly loved, clothe yourselves*
> *with compassion, kindness, humility, gentleness and patience.*
>
> COLOSSIANS 3:12

Because we have trusted Christ, we have been "set apart" from the world, unto the Lord. That is the meaning of the word "holy." We are not our own; we belong completely to Him (1 Cor. 6:19–20). Just as the marriage ceremony sets apart a man and a woman for each other exclusively, so salvation sets believers apart exclusively for Jesus Christ. Would it not be a horrible thing, at the end of a wedding, to see the groom run off with the maid of honor? It is just as horrible to contemplate Christians living for the world and the flesh.

When unbelievers sin, they are creatures breaking the laws of the holy Creator and Judge. But when we Christians sin, we are children of God breaking the loving heart of our heavenly Father. Love is the strongest motivating power in the world. As we grow in our love for God, we will grow in our desire to obey Him and to walk in the newness of life that is ours in Christ.

Applying God's Truth:

1. In what ways are you "set apart" from the world?

2. Can you think of any additional ways you need to be set apart in order to show more devotion to Christ than to worldly concerns?

3. If your relationship with Jesus were a marriage, what kind of shape would it be in? If it were a physical parent-child relationship, do you think it would be a good one overall? Explain.

Day 22

Let Peace Rule

Read Colossians 3:15

Let the peace of Christ rule in your hearts, since as members
of one body you were called to peace. And be thankful.
COLOSSIANS 3:15

In the Greek games there were judges (we would call them "umpires") who rejected contestants who were not qualified and who disqualified those who broke the rules. The peace of God is the "umpire" in our believing hearts. When we obey the will of God, we have His peace within; but when we step out of His will (even unintentionally), we lose His peace.

If we have peace in our hearts, we will be at peace with others in the church. We are called to one body, and our relationship in that body must be one of harmony and peace. If we are out of the will of God, we are certain to bring discord and disharmony to the church. Jonah thought he was at peace, when actually his sins created a storm! (Jonah 1–4).

When we Christians lose the peace of God, we begin to go off in directions that are out of the will of God. We turn to the things of the world and the flesh to compensate for our lack of peace within. We try to escape, but we cannot escape *ourselves!* It is only when we confess our sins, claim God's forgiveness, and do God's will that we experience God's peace within.

Applying God's Truth:

1. How do you feel when an umpire makes what you feel is a bad call against your favorite team? How do you feel when God expects something from you that you feel is unfair?

2. Have you ever experienced a false peace (like Jonah's)? How long did it last? What were the results?

3. What situations are you facing today for which you need to experience God's peace?

Day 23

Sing Along

Read Colossians 3:16–17

Let the word of Christ dwell in you richly as you teach and admonish one another with all wisdom, and as you sing psalms, hymns and spiritual songs with gratitude in your hearts to God.

COLOSSIANS 3:16

Psalms were the songs taken from the Old Testament. For centuries, the churches in the English-speaking world sang only metrical versions of the Psalms. I am glad to see today a return to the singing of Scripture, especially the Psalms. Hymns were songs of praise to God written by believers but not taken from the book of Psalms. The church today has a rich heritage of hymnody which, I fear, is being neglected. Spiritual songs were expressions of biblical truth other than in psalms and hymns. When we sing a hymn, we address the Lord; when we sing a spiritual song, we address each other.

Someone has said that a successful Christian life involves attention to three books: God's Book, the Bible; the pocketbook; and the hymnbook. I agree. I often use a hymnal in my devotional time, to help express my praise to God. As we believers grow in our knowledge of the Word, we will want to grow in our expression of praise. We will learn to appreciate the great hymns of the church, the gospel songs, and the spiritual songs that teach spiritual truths. To sing only the elementary songs of the faith is to rob ourselves of spiritual enrichment.

Applying God's Truth:

1. What are some of your favorite hymns and spiritual songs? Why?

2. How important is singing in your church worship?

3. How important are hymns and spiritual songs in your personal worship?

Day 24

Love and Submission

Read Colossians 3:18–19

> *Wives, submit to your husbands, as is fitting in the Lord. Husbands,*
> *love your wives and do not be harsh with them.*
> COLOSSIANS 3:18–19

Paul did not address the wives first because they were neediest! The gospel radically changed the position of women in the Roman world. It gave them a new freedom and stature that some of them were unable to handle, and for this reason Paul admonished them.

We must not think of "submission" as "slavery" or "subjugation." The word comes from the military vocabulary and simply means "arrangement under rank." The fact that one soldier is a private and another is a colonel does not mean that one is necessarily *better* than the other. It only means that they have different ranks.

God does all things "in a fitting and orderly way" (1 Cor. 14:40). If He did not have a chain of command in society, we would have chaos. The fact that the woman is to submit to her husband does not suggest that the man is better than the woman. It only means that the man has the responsibility of headship and leadership in the home.

Headship is not dictatorship or lordship. It is loving leadership. In fact, both the husband and the wife must be submitted to *the Lord* and to *each other* (Eph. 5:21). It is a mutual respect under the lordship of Jesus Christ.

Applying God's Truth:

1. Do you think there are ever times when it is appropriate for a wife to refuse to submit to her husband? Explain.

2. Of the two commands Paul gives in Colossians 3:18–19, which do you think is harder to obey? Why?

3. In what area(s) do you find it hardest to submit to someone else? To God? When is it easiest?

Day 25

Kid Stuff

Read Colossians 3:20—4:1

Children, obey your parents in everything, for this pleases the Lord.
COLOSSIANS 3:20

John H. Starkey was a violent British criminal. He murdered his own wife, then was convicted for the crime and executed. The officials asked General William Booth, founder of the Salvation Army, to conduct Starkey's funeral. Booth faced as ugly and mean a crowd as he had ever seen in his life, but his first words stopped them and held them: "John H. Starkey never had a praying mother!"

Children have rights, but they also have responsibilities; and their foremost responsibility is to obey. They are to obey "in everything" and not simply in those things that please themselves. Will their parents ever ask them to do something that is wrong? Not if the parents are submitted to the Lord and to one another, and not if they love each other and their children.

Children who do not learn to obey their parents are not likely to grow up obeying any authority. They will defy their teachers, the police, their employers, and anyone else who tries to exercise authority over them. The breakdown in authority in our society reflects the breakdown of authority in the home.

Applying God's Truth:

1. How is children's obedience to parents significant in regard to their eventual obedience to God?

2. Can you tell whether a child (who is a stranger to you) is obedient or not? If so, how?

3. When people observe you, do you think they can tell whether you are an obedient child of God? How?

Day 26

Devoted to Devotions

Read Colossians 4:2

Devote yourselves to prayer, being watchful and thankful.
COLOSSIANS 4:2

Prayer and worship are perhaps the highest uses of the gift of speech. It has well been said that the purpose of prayer is not to get our will done in heaven, but to get God's will done on earth. Prayer is not telling God what to do or what to give. Prayer is asking God for that which He wants to do and give, according to His will (1 John 5:14–15).

As we read the Word and fellowship with our Father, we discover His will and then boldly ask Him to do what He has planned. Richard Trench (1807–1886), archbishop of Dublin, said it perfectly: "Prayer is not overcoming God's reluctance; it is laying hold of His willingness."

Of course, it is possible to pray in our hearts and never use the gift of speech, but we are using words even if we don't say them audibly. True prayer must first come from the heart, whether the words are spoken or not.

Applying God's Truth:

1. On a scale of 1 (least) to 10 (most), how intently would you say you devote yourself to prayer?

2. What is one portion of God's will for your life that you have recently determined? Have you verbally affirmed it in prayer?

3. As you pray, in what ways are you "watchful"? In what ways are you "thankful"?

Day 27

A Clear Proclamation

Read Colossians 4:3–4

> *Pray for us, too, that God may open a door for our message,*
> *so that we may proclaim the mystery of Christ, for which I am*
> *in chains. Pray that I may proclaim it clearly, as I should.*
>
> COLOSSIANS 4:3–4

A visitor at Spurgeon's Tabernacle in London was being shown around the building by the pastor, Charles Haddon Spurgeon.

"Would you like to see the powerhouse of this ministry?" Spurgeon asked, as he showed the man into a lower auditorium. "It is here that we get our power, for while I am preaching upstairs, hundreds of my people are in this room praying." Is it any wonder that God blessed Spurgeon's preaching of the Word?

You, as a church member, can assist your pastor in the preaching of the Word by praying for him. Never say to your pastor, "Well, the least I can do is to pray for you." The *most* you can do is to pray! Pray for your pastor as he prepares the Word, studies, and meditates. Pray that the Holy Spirit will give deeper insights into the truths of the Word. Pray too that your pastor will practice the Word that he preaches so that it will be real in his own life. As he preaches the message, pray that the Spirit will give him freedom of utterance and that the Word will reach into hearts and minds in a powerful way. (And it wouldn't hurt to pray for other church leaders, too.)

Applying God's Truth:

1. What are some specific ways that you can more effectively pray for your pastor?

2. In addition to the pastor, who are some other people in your church who need your prayers today?

3. What things may interfere with the "clear" presentation of the gospel? How can prayer help deal with such interferences?

Day 28

Salty Talk

Read Colossians 4:5–6

> *Let your conversation be always full of grace, seasoned with salt,*
> *so that you may know how to answer everyone.*
>
> COLOSSIANS 4:6

Christians in general, and Christian leaders in particular, must have "a good reputation with outsiders" (1 Tim. 3:7). When members of a church are calling a new pastor, they ought to investigate his testimony among his neighbors and the businessmen who know him. Even though unsaved people are in the dark spiritually, they have a great deal of discernment when it comes to the things of this life. It is unfortunate when members of a church call a pastor who has not paid his bills and has left behind a bad witness to unsaved people.

It is not enough simply to walk wisely and carefully before unbelievers. We must also *talk* with them and share the gospel message with them. But we must take care that our speech is controlled by *grace*, so that it points to Christ and glorifies the Lord. This means we must have grace in our hearts (Col. 3:16), because it is from the heart that the mouth speaks (Matt. 12:34). With grace in our hearts and on our lips, we will be faithful witnesses and not judges or prosecuting attorneys!

Applying God's Truth:

1. Can you think of a recent scandal involving a prominent

Christian figure? What was the response of the non-Christians in your area?

2. What do you think it means to let your speech be "seasoned with salt"?

3. What people can you think of whose Christian testimony is that of "faithful witnesses"? Do you know any "judges"? Any "prosecuting attorneys"?

Day 29

Name Recognition

Read Colossians 4:7–13

My fellow prisoner Aristarchus sends you his greetings.
Colossians 4:10

Aristarchus was identified as Paul's "fellow prisoner" and also as one of Paul's "fellow workers" (Philem. v. 24). Aristarchus was from Macedonia and was one of Paul's traveling companions (Acts 19:29). He was originally from Thessalonica (20:4) and had willingly risked his life in the Ephesian riot (19:28–41). He sailed with Paul to Rome (27:2), which meant that he also experienced the storm and shipwreck that Luke so graphically described in Acts 27.

Aristarchus stayed with Paul no matter what the circumstances were—a riot in Ephesus, a voyage, a storm, or even a prison. It is not likely that Aristarchus was an official Roman prisoner. "Fellow prisoner" probably means that Aristarchus shared Paul's confinement with him so that he could be a help and comfort to the apostle. He was a voluntary prisoner for the sake of Jesus Christ and the gospel.

Paul could not have accomplished all that he did apart from the assistance of his friends. Aristarchus stands out as one of the greatest of Paul's helpers. He did not look for an easy task. He did not run when the going got tough. He suffered with Paul and labored with Paul.

Applying God's Truth:

1. Since Aristarchus was so supportive of Paul, why do you think he isn't better known?

2. Can you think of people who serve God faithfully yet whose efforts frequently go unnoticed?

3. What might you do to recognize the work of the Aristarchus-like people in your church or ministry?

Day 30

Which Master Will You Choose?

Read Colossians 4:14–18

Our dear friend Luke, the doctor, and Demas send greetings.
COLOSSIANS 4:14

Demas is mentioned only three times in Paul's letters, and these three references tell a sad story. First, Paul calls him "Demas … [one of] my fellow workers" and links him with three good men—Mark, Aristarchus, and Luke (Philem. v. 24). Then, Paul simply calls him "Demas," with no special word of identification or commendation (Col. 4:14). But in the third reference Paul tells us what became of him: "Demas, because he loved this world, has deserted me" (2 Tim. 4:10).

At one point in his life, John Mark had forsaken Paul, but he was reclaimed and restored. Demas forsook Paul and apparently was never reclaimed. His sin was that he "loved this present world" (2 Tim. 4:10 KJV). The word "world" refers to the whole system of things that runs this world, or "society without God."

We Christians today can succumb to the world just as Demas did. How easy it is to maintain a religious veneer, while all the time we are living for the things of this world. Demas thought that he could serve two masters (Matt. 6:24; Luke 16:13), but eventually he had to make a decision; unfortunately, he made the wrong decision.

It must have hurt Paul greatly when Demas forsook him. It also hurt the work of the Lord, for there never has been a time when the laborers were many (Matt. 9:37; Luke 10:2). This decision hurt

Demas most of all, for he wasted his life on that which could never last.

Applying God's Truth:

1. Do you know any believers who, like Demas, seem in danger of forsaking their spiritual commitments? If so, is there any way for you to help them?

2. What tends to lure *you* away from the faith—if you aren't careful?

3. Based on what you have read in Colossians, what can you do to stay faithful when you are tempted to wander away from God?